NAKED
VALUE

NAKED VALUE

**Six Things Every Business Leader
Needs to Know About Resources,
Innovation & Competition**

Howard J. Brown

Kristin Aldred Cheek

Kathryn Lewis

*d***MASS** Media
dMASS.net

Naked Value and dMASS are trademarks of Howard J. Brown.

To order copies of this book (electronic or print-on-demand),
visit dMASS.net online or write to:

dMASS
800 Village Walk
Suite 156
Guilford, CT 06437

Library of Congress Control Number: 2012937718

Brown, Howard J., Kristin Aldred Cheek, and Kathryn Lewis.

*Naked Value: Six Things Every Business Leader Needs
to Know About Resources, Innovation & Competition.*

1st edition. Guilford: dMASS Media, 2012.
Includes notes.

ISBN 978-0-9854474-0-3

Cover design by Daniela C. Nelke.
Illustrations by Carlos Morales and Daniela C. Nelke.
Book design by Sue Balcer of JustYourType.biz.

Contents

Acknowledgments

WE OWE THANKS to many people who have helped make this book possible.

We are grateful to our patient and thoughtful readers and colleagues Lionel Wolberger, Ali Abate, Jennifer Malone, Mimi Egan, Justin Brown, Andrew Borneman, and Karen Gangel.

To Carlos Morales and Daniela C. Nelke for their professional assistance in helping us convey dMASS ideas visually.

To Mark Loeffler, Gregor Barnum, Cary Krosinsky, Nicholas Hill, Kelvin Roth, and Carol Singer Neuvelt and the staff at the National Association of Environmental Management (NAEM) for their encouragement and collaboration throughout our successful first year.

We are all grateful to our families and friends for their support and encouragement.

We would also like to recognize R. Buckminster Fuller, whose lifework inspired our early discussions on dMASS thinking.

About the Authors

Howard J. Brown has founded several business ventures to help companies align good business and environmental practices. For more than 20 years as CEO of Resource Planning & Management Systems (RPM), Inc., in New Haven, Connecticut, he worked with major companies such as Duracell, Avery Dennison, Mobil, GE, John Deere, Whirlpool, Warner Lambert, and Pfizer to establish or enhance their environmental practices and performance. His proven techniques are still state-of-the-art at universities and corporations around the globe today, and he continues to push the leading edge with new ideas. He was a founder of The World Game Institute and taught at Yale and at Wesleyan University. Howard was also student and colleague of R. Buckminster Fuller and is an authority on the social and economic implications of Fuller's work.

    Kristin Aldred Cheek is a sustainable business practitioner focused on helping businesses identify the benefits customers desire from products and understand the relationship between resources, products, and value. Her experience includes advising companies on energy efficiency and resource performance and managing communications for companies engaged in environmental cleanup projects. She has expertise in social science research and has conducted studies on public participation in natural resource management and on the economic impacts of natural resource use.

Kathryn Lewis is an entrepreneur with expertise in business system analysis and performance optimization. Kathryn has written about resources and their relationship to metrics, waste minimization, logistics, and supply chain management and has presented dMASS research and innovations to audiences in Europe and the United States. Kathryn's previous work includes developing an online network regarding energy harvesting and conducting marketing analyses for a global logistics company.

Preface

THIS BOOK IS ABOUT naked value—what it is, why it's becoming the defining issue of our times, and how it will change your company's products and services.[1] It's about using resource performance to increase your products' value and improve their position in a competitive marketplace.

The way business leaders think about value and costs is about to change dramatically. A product's real value is determined by the relationship between the benefits that people gain by using that product and the resources it takes to deliver those benefits.

Resource performance is a relatively simple but powerful new way to measure and improve product value. It's a key indicator of a product's profit potential, environmental impacts and risks, and competitive position. Resource performance also reflects a product's vulnerability to volatility in resource prices and supplies.

By making resource performance part of your mindset, you can avoid many of the threats to your business and discover opportunities you probably never imagined.

The team at dMASS.net inventories cutting-edge research, technology innovations, and new business models that companies can use to improve their products' value. The examples we share range from prototypes and experiments to solutions already on the market. They include ideas that change how companies design, manufacture, distribute, and reclaim products. They also include new business models for finding and delivering a product's ultimate value—its naked value—to customers.

THE WAY BUSINESS LEADERS THINK ABOUT VALUE AND COSTS IS ABOUT TO CHANGE DRAMATICALLY

Taken together, the examples we've identified confirm that a design revolution is under way around the world, one that's changing the product marketplace. This revolution will enable economic prosperity to expand using a fraction of the resources currently needed to support each human being.

We've developed an approach that offers design and business strategies to help companies adapt to a changing business environment. The dMASS approach leverages the latest knowledge and technology to improve the resource performance of products, deliver naked value to customers, and measure progress. Resource performance improvements are evident throughout history in nearly every product category, industry, or research field, from the aerospace industry to medicine. Current sustainable business initiatives, such as biomimicry, cradle-to-cradle design, and collaborative consumption, are just the latest methods for doing better with less. dMASS offers a broad, systematic approach to help businesses intentionally pursue the kind of innovation that will drastically alter the relationship between the use of resources and the production of wealth.

Naked Value is the first book from dMASS.net. In the book, we introduce six critical concepts that businesses need to succeed in a resource-constrained world. We also present a simplified approach to help companies achieve naked value. We use concrete examples to demonstrate:

- How customer value and value delivery are changing
- Why every business is at risk from competitors with entirely new and surprising ways to deliver value to customers
- Why resources are central to every business decision and to innovation
- How seemingly disparate trends in everything from supply chain management to emerging business models are connected
- Why every business leader should monitor advances in biology, nanotechnology, and other scientific fields

In the course of our work we've found countless opportunities hidden in the immense problems facing businesses today. We're excited to share what we've learned. We wrote this book for business leaders, designers, architects, engineers, and investors. You are in a position to influence the design and delivery of products. The book contains the most important information about resource performance presented in a concise format. In other words, our intent was to deliver naked value. We hope you find the ideas in this book useful in your endeavors.

Howard J. Brown
Kristin Aldred Cheek
Kathryn Lewis

NAKED
VALUE

Introduction:
The Naked Future

The Trend

ON NOVEMBER 1, 1999, something happened in the financial world that was a sign of the radical changes in store for business and ultimately for the global economy. Microsoft Corporation joined the Dow Jones Industrial Average, while at the same time, large industrial companies, like Chevron, Goodyear, and Union Carbide, were removed.

The Dow is composed of a select group of companies that has come to collectively symbolize the industrial sector of the American economy. But most of Microsoft's products were not industrial by then-accepted definitions of the term. Unlike most other companies that made up the Dow in 1999, Microsoft didn't have significant environmental management costs or risks, hazardous waste liabilities, fossil fuel problems, or worker safety problems.

It didn't have to worry about capital expenditures for factories or heavy machinery and it certainly didn't have to worry about commodity prices and resource shortages. The company was earning billions of dollars in revenue per year, yet most of its products were essentially weightless.

Microsoft's products were extremely valuable to the

Words to Know

Benefits result from using products or services. They contribute to a customer's wealth or well-being. The relationship between benefits and resource use determines a product or service's *value*.

Resources include all minerals, metals, fuels, water, and other materials.

Waste typically refers to materials sent to landfill, effluent released to water treatment, air emissions, and other by-products of production that have no presumed value. The dMASS definition of waste is more expansive. Waste includes any resources used that aren't essential to delivering benefits to customers. It includes much of the materials that make up a product and its packaging, as well as resources lost in processing.

company's customers. Virtually every business needed and wanted them. The products had naked value, which is to say they performed an important function for customers yet they contained little of the mass traditionally associated with manufacturing products. The products required only minimal amounts of materials and fuels to deliver them to customers.

Resource performance is what determines a product's value. It refers to the relationship between all the material inputs in the design, manufacture, and delivery of a product or service and the benefits customers derive from that product or service. Resource performance improvements alter this relationship to deliver more benefits using fewer tons of inputs.

Naked value is the essence that remains in a product or service after stripping away all unneeded resources. It's the pure benefit customers seek, without waste and without material resources that don't contribute to wealth or well-being. It reflects the highest level of resource performance for a product.

dMASS refers to the overall strategy of improving resource performance in pursuit of naked value.

The trend toward drastic reductions in the use of resources to make and deliver products may have taken off with software,

<CUSTOMERS WANT

NAKED VALUE>>

but it is now spreading to every market and industrial sector. It's not an information technology phenomenon. It's a technological design revolution. To succeed in the coming decades, businesses will need to understand it, embrace it, and use it to their advantage.

The Challenge

Customers want naked value. They want the pure benefits of products. At the same time, every business faces heightened resource-related risks, including growing global demands and mounting price, supply, and other pressures. Industry leaders in the naked value economy will be those who deliver the most benefits to customers with the fewest resources.

Fortunately, rapidly advancing materials science, biology, and technology are revolutionizing businesses' ability to do better with less. New discoveries in science and engineering are making it more feasible to rearrange energy at the level of individual atoms and molecules, yielding new materials with previously unimaginable characteristics. These materials have the capability to drastically reduce the amount of all resources needed to deliver benefits. Companies are developing products that deliver light without light bulbs, portable power without batteries, warmth without thick insulation or boilers, bacteria-safe surfaces without chemicals, and clean clothes without detergent.

The convergence of knowledge, technology, and resource trends are redefining manufacturing, environmental management, and business in general. The keys to prosperity for an individual business or for an entire economy are different today than they were in the past. Adapting your business is the key to managing risk and to remaining competitive. Starting the change now is necessary for success.

> COMPANIES ARE DEVELOPING PRODUCTS THAT DELIVER LIGHT WITHOUT LIGHT BULBS, PORTABLE POWER WITHOUT BATTERIES, WARMTH WITHOUT THICK INSULATION OR BOILERS, BACTERIA-SAFE SURFACES WITHOUT CHEMICALS, AND CLEAN CLOTHES WITHOUT DETERGENT

Getting Started

This book contains six essential principles that can form the basis for your dMASS business strategy. They are:

1. Every business decision is about resources
2. Waste isn't the problem
3. No one wants your products
4. Innovation has direction
5. You don't know your competition
6. Your products are mostly waste

The chart below, which appears again in later chapters, is a simplified illustration of naked value concepts. It's a tool that can be used for developing a dMASS strategy and for tracking progress toward achieving naked value.

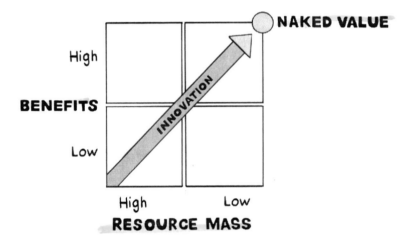

Figure 1: Resource Performance, Innovation & Naked Value

Innovation today is about delivering more benefits with fewer resources, with the ultimate goal of achieving naked value. Any resource performance improvements that reduce resource mass or increase benefits are important steps in the right direction.

The final chapter of *Naked Value* offers a brief guide to help you begin to develop a dMASS plan for your products. Included at the back of the book are several exercises to help you practice dMASS thinking for your business and your products.

Reading *Naked Value*

As you read, think about how to apply the ideas in this book to your business. Keep these central questions in mind: Why do customers buy your products or services? What benefits do they seek? What business are you really in? This book includes additional questions and exercises to prime your thinking; more are available online at dMASS.net.

1

Every Business Decision Is About Resources

POPULATION GROWTH and resource use are the most significant factors that will force fundamental change in your business, including the way you design, manufacture, and distribute your products. They've already profoundly changed the world in which you operate, even if their impact is not yet widely and fully recognized, and they will only continue to grow in importance.

Population Growth Is a Business Issue

Population growth isn't just a human interest story limited to the realm of policymakers and non-profits, nor is it just a challenge for the future. It's a major business issue now, and it's the force behind significant risks for every business.

Global population more than doubled in five decades during the last century, ballooning from 2.5 billion to more than 6 billion between 1950 and 2000.[2] It only took 12 more years to add another billion people. Such a dramatic change surely affects business. In business, population growth is often framed as an opportunity; more people means more opportunity to sell goods and services. But because of the relationship between population growth and resource use, the situation has become much more complicated.

Population and Resource Use Are Intertwined

More people on the planet means increased demand and competition for resources. Though population growth tends to stabilize with economic development (childbirth rates decrease as economic security increases), per capita resource use traditionally rises alongside economic development, so more economic development also means more competition for resources.

Growing demand in the face of constrained supplies creates resource price volatility and conflict over unreliable supplies. So, while your markets grow, and perhaps demand for your products grows, the resources you need to operate your business become more expensive and less accessible.

The relationship between rising economic development and rising resource use needs to change. Changing it through resource performance is the basis of the opportunities we'll discuss in later chapters.

It's All About Resources

The upshot is that resources are now at the heart of nearly every major challenge facing businesses and even entire economies around the globe. They constitute the primary factor shaping businesses for the foreseeable future. Though there's some evidence of moderate gains in resource efficiency, total resource use is expected to continue to grow.[3] Global water use tripled during the past 30 years,[4] and many vital resources, from phosphorus fertilizer to fuels, are under substantial pressure.[5] The United Nations predicts that overall use could triple by 2050.[6] As overall global resource use climbs further, resource security, reliability, and pricing only become more crucial to business.

> RESOURCES ARE NOW AT THE HEART OF NEARLY EVERY MAJOR CHALLENGE FACING BUSINESSES AND EVEN ENTIRE ECONOMIES AROUND THE GLOBE

Resource security is already a serious business problem. The British Geological Survey now publishes a "Risk List"[7] ranking 52 economically important elements based on risk to supply. The list takes into account growing demand and increasing competition for metals and minerals, as well as the distribution and location of those resources, and the political stability of the countries where they are found. In 2010, China, which produces more than 90 percent of the world's rare earth elements,[8] temporarily suspended shipments of rare earths to Japan.[9] Companies rely on these materials to manufacture an array of high-tech products, including auto parts. The supply disruption may have been due to a diplomatic dispute or to China's recently imposed global export quota on rare earths. Either way, the disruption elevated the problem of resource security for all businesses.

Even while sales increase, profits can decline as resource costs climb.

Water use is another challenge at the forefront for businesses. More than one-third of global companies surveyed by Ceres, a coalition of investors and public interest groups, have experienced negative impacts related to water, including increased costs and operational disruptions.[10]

Today, businesses are making major decisions based on the growing, strategic importance of resources. For instance, companies are investing in research regarding resource supplies. They are taking direct responsibility for the stewardship of raw materials. They are investing in the research and development of substitute materials. Most importantly, from the dMASS perspective, companies are purposefully using design and technology to cut materials from their products and packaging. Business leaders in every market need to vigilantly attend to these trends or they risk losing their competitive advantage.

Circumstances Have Changed

Before we discuss examples of product re-designs, new technologies that make those re-designs more feasible, or significant business model changes, there are three important aspects of resource risks that are important to understand.

First, current resource constraints and pressures are not a temporary phenomenon. Current conditions are due to the size and continued expansion of the global population, the existing relationship between economic development and resource use, and rising standards of living. Jeremy Grantham, a prominent investor and respected business analyst, argues that current conditions reflect a permanent change in the global economic environment rather than cyclical economic phenomenon. He asserts that the world isn't just approaching peak oil, but "peak everything."[11] In

> « BUSINESSES ARE MAKING MAJOR DECISIONS BASED ON THE GROWING, STRATEGIC IMPORTANCE OF RESOURCES »

a 2011 article titled "Time to Wake Up: Days of Abundant Resources and Falling Prices Are over Forever," he states:

> The world is using up its natural resources at an alarming rate, and this has caused a permanent shift in their value. We all need to adjust our behavior to this new environment. It would help if we did it quickly.
>
> The prices of all important commodities except oil declined for 100 years until 2002, by an average of 70%. From 2002 until now, this entire decline was erased by a bigger price surge than occurred during World War II. Statistically, most commodities are now so far away from their former downward trend that it makes it very probable that the old trend has changed, that there is in fact a paradigm shift, perhaps the most important economic event since the Industrial Revolution.
>
> From now on, price pressure and shortages of resources will be a permanent feature of our lives.[12]

Second, environmental regulations, along with customer demands for corporate responsibility and transparency, are symptoms, not causes of, resource-related risks. This is an important point because it affects how businesses respond to potential risks. Regulations and demands for transparency are the result of the growing demand for resources within an essentially limited system. They have accelerated due to tremendous gains in scientific knowledge and access to environmental and corporate information.

Finally, dMASS thinking applies to all resources and to all businesses. Resource constraints and pressures affect more than oil, rare earths, precious metals, or any specific commodity used by a particular industry, in part because so many resources are connected. For example, acquiring, moving, and processing any material requires fuels. Likewise, acquiring, moving, and processing fuels requires an array of materials. The ubiquitous nature of water also shows why dMASS thinking is relevant for every business. Fresh water is a tool employed in manufacturing, a critical component of the agricultural industry, a major factor in power generation, and an ingredient in everything from detergents to processed foods. It's an integral part of product supply chains. Not surprisingly, water-related risks are among the first resource risks to have caught the attention of investors.[13]

The point is that circumstances have changed. You're operating your business today in a world that's fundamentally different than it was even a decade ago. And changed circumstances call for a change in strategy.

Companies Are Adapting

Many companies are altering strategies, products, and even business models to cope with resource risks. Familiar first steps in pursuing naked value include increasing product and operational efficiency, product lightweighting, dematerialization, and using recycled and renewable materials. The dMASS approach goes beyond mere efficiency and places resource management at the center of business decisions. It calls for significant resource performance improvements that require rethinking a product's design altogether. Evidence of a shift toward this type of thinking exists in resource stewardship, product redesign, research and development, and much more.

CHANGED CIRCUMSTANCES CALL FOR A CHANGE IN STRATEGY

For example, in resource stewardship, companies around the globe are taking a more active role in ensuring the sustainable management of resources, working directly with farmers, putting conservation programs in place, and investing in research. Coca-Cola has been collecting data regarding water trends and risks for the past several years. The company started the project because water is the lifeblood of its business and needs to be managed strategically, similar to human, financial, or any other important business investment. In the midst of their water-related work, company executives realized the strategic importance of water to the entire global economy. So the company shared its water data with the World Resource Institute for use in the non-profit's Aqueduct program, which provides interactive mapping of local water risks across the globe.[14] Note that Coca-Cola's project is about more than using water efficiently or being a responsible corporate citizen. Water is vital to the company's existence. Coca-Cola's actions support its primary goals for managing the business and managing risk.

In addition to changing their management of raw materials, businesses are altering resource management through changes in product designs. For instance, in response to supply risks, Toyota began developing an efficient electric motor that does not require rare earth elements.[15] The company also launched a new effort to recycle rare earth elements from magnets and to recover nickel from batteries.[16] Pepsi, motivated by volatile oil prices, is working to eliminate petroleum from its bottles and is planning to use bio-waste from its various product lines to make bottles. Many other manufacturers and retailers are also cutting plastic and weight from packaging for the same reason.[17]

There's no doubt that businesses are changing their strategies to adapt to new circumstances. But this is just the beginning. Emerging research, new technologies, and creative thinking are making it possible to reduce resource use much more dramatically.

2

Waste Isn't the Problem

WASTE PROBLEMS ARE best solved by focusing on the resources used for products rather than focusing on the waste itself. The significant push in business right now to reduce waste is somewhat misdirected because it generally deals with waste on the "back end" of operations, where it's thought of as an unwanted by-product generated at the end of a process. A better approach acknowledges just how closely resource inputs and a company's outputs are related. Before we explain this approach, we need to look briefly at current views about waste management and how they developed.

A Very Short History of Waste Management

Until fairly recently, resource use and waste weren't much more than an afterthought for businesses. Resources were abundant and accessible. Competition for them was relatively low in relation to supply. Resource problems were largely regionalized. The cost of using virgin materials was low enough that materials recovery was understandably absent from many companies' priority lists. The by-products of industry were simply discarded. The costs and consequences of these actions weren't well understood.

Then, population growth accelerated. The number of people living near extraction, production, and waste sites rose. Knowledge of the negative ecological and human health impacts from industrial activities spread. Concentrated, high-quality supplies of many materials, once thought to be endless, became constrained. Conflict over the conservation and availability of resources increased. In the midst of these circumstances, several deeply flawed myths took hold: the idea that environment and business are at odds, the notion that protecting one inevitably means harm to the other, and the belief that substantial waste is somehow a necessary by-product of doing business. This way of looking at environment and business led to a general misunderstanding of resource-related business risks and to missed opportunities.

The Business of Rearranging Our Environment

Let's look at a very simple illustration of the relationship between the environment, products, resources, and waste. Our biosphere, the thin envelope surrounding the planet in which life exists, is finite. Except for incoming sunlight, the material resources here on this planet are what we have to work with. From this environment, we dig up, rearrange, process, and transport resources. Businesses use these resources to create products, from major infrastructure to buildings, appliances, clothing, and computers. These products are the tools that each of us use to derive some kind of benefit for health, security, and well-being. Products are essentially our environment, temporarily rearranged. Every part of your business is dependent on our environment and a supply of resources in some way. Every component of your business was once part of our environment and eventually will be again. Every action by your business has effects that reverberate throughout our environment.

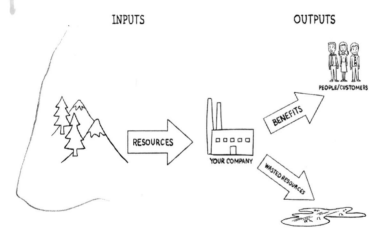

Figure 2: A Simple Illustration of the Relationship Between the Environment, Products, Resources, and Waste

Businesses use resources from our environment to create products. Waste includes any resources used that aren't essential to delivering benefits to customers, including materials in products and packaging, as well as resources lost during processing. A company's products, its waste, and all of its physical assets are rearranged resources. The primary output of business is really *benefits* that people want, not the material aspect of products.

The truth is that every business operates within the earth's environment. The success of your company depends on our environment and its resources. No company can expect to compete under today's circumstances by managing waste as a by-product at the back end of business operations. You have to pay attention to inputs at the front end. You have to manage resources.

ALL WASTES ARE SIMPLY RESOURCES 'LOST' IN THE COURSE OF DOING BUSINESS

Let's look more closely at waste. For now, we'll use the conventional idea of waste: materials sent to landfill, effluent released to water treatment, air emissions, and other by-products that have no presumed value. All wastes are simply resources "lost" in the course of doing business.

Consider an oil spill, like the 2010 Deepwater Horizon disaster in the Gulf of Mexico. Millions of gallons of oil were lost from the drill site. All of it, captured as intended, would have been processed and sold as a valuable product. During that processing, some of it inevitably would have spilled. Some more might have spilled during transport. Finally, some of it would have been released into the atmosphere after it was sold and burned. Nevertheless, it's fundamentally the same resource whether it's in the ground, in a tank, dispersed in water, or in the air.

Resources can either contribute to or diminish human well-being, depending on their form. Resources are valuable when they are in a form that can easily be used and transformed into wealth. But they become harmful pollution when they're released where they don't belong or in a form that disrupts natural systems. Resources can be important assets that enable businesses to operate, or they can be expensive liabilities that increase operating costs.

FOCUS ON MANAGING RESOURCE INPUTS INSTEAD OF MANAGING THE CONSEQUENCES OF USING THOSE RESOURCES

The legal definitions of pollution have shifted over time, and they will shift further as conditions and awareness continue to change. However, the simple reality that wastes and pollution are lost resources will not change. Your business pays to have resources mined, processed, shipped around the world, formed into finished materials, and distributed. Every resource your company wastes, it pays for. Your company then pays again to manage waste, clean up spills, and purchase new resources to replace what was lost.

The Switch to Front-End Management

The most important message to businesses is this: *Focus on managing resource inputs instead of managing the consequences of using those resources.* The best way to do this is simple: limit resource use in the first place. If you don't use it, you can't spill it. You also don't have to pay for it, transport it, store it, clean it up, or take responsibility for it at the end of its useful life as a product. The best business strategies now are the ones that focus more on reducing inputs than on reducing unintended outputs. Reducing inputs ultimately enhances the asset value of your business and the value of your products.

A simple change in metrics can help businesses shift from managing by-products to managing resource inputs. After all, you get what you measure. Not surprisingly, measuring tons of recycled material results in more tons of recycled material, not necessarily a decrease in the total tons of materials used. If your goal is to use fewer resources in the first place, that's what you should be measuring.

Unfortunately, the present status of environmental metrics is far from ideal. Most metrics are designed for external stakeholders, like investors, NGOs, and ratings firms. They are also exceedingly complicated. They're rarely useful for strategic planning or for reducing resource use. They inadvertently divert companies' efforts away from improving product performance to improving reporting scores.

When your company purchases resources that don't ultimately contribute to benefits for customers, this needlessly ties up resources. This drives up business costs in the long run, as it adds to demand for resources. When these resources are released back into the environment as waste, they can directly harm people, the same people businesses rely on to buy their products.

In the end, the relationship between resources used and benefits delivered to customers is what matters most. This is what you need to measure. We'll explore this important concept in more detail in the next chapter. First, let's look at several examples of what companies are doing today to reduce waste.

Waste Management Strategies Today

The view of waste in business has shifted a great deal over the last two decades. Today, more companies are operating with the understanding that "waste" is in fact valuable. Waste management has become a priority for many. This is playing out in several different ways. Some companies are using inputs that are materials castoff from other industries. Some are making products that are reusable, recyclable, more durable, or easily deconstructed. Others are minimizing packaging and redesigning products and processes to minimize scrap and by-products.

InterfaceFLOR is one corporate leader in waste reduction. Guided by the principle of "eliminating the concept of waste," the company changed its carpet-tile dyeing and designs to reduce waste during installation, installed sensors to reduce water and manufacturing waste, patented new machinery that produces less scrap during manufacturing, started taking back used carpet from its customers for reprocessing, and began pursuing zero waste at its facilities.[18,19]

Zero waste strategies often save money and reduce environmental impacts at the same time, so they can be a way to align an organization's financial and environmental goals.[20] Zero waste typically follows the reduce-reuse-recycle framework, with some conversion of waste to energy through incineration. Major companies like General Motors, Proctor & Gamble, and Xerox are pursuing zero waste strategies at their facilities. General Motors, for one, is turning its waste streams into product components and reuses or recycles 97 percent of waste at more than half of its plants.[21] Materials exchange, where the by-products of one company's process serve as the feedstock for a different company, is another effective tactic for diverting waste. Companies are also taking responsibility for product materials at the end of the products' useful lives. For example, Sprint plans to recover the equivalent of 90 percent of its products for reuse and recycling by 2017.[22]

What's Next for Waste

There's evidence that the definitions of waste and pollution are expanding. For instance, just recently concerns have arisen about the unintended environmental consequences from pharmaceutical products. The United States has a drug take-back program that enables people to dispose of unwanted and unused prescription drugs.[23] But in the case of medicines, "waste" doesn't include only discarded surplus or expired material. A lot of medicine reenters our environment through excretion and wastewater.

What about other products that are eventually dispersed not into managed waste streams but into diffuse ones? Tons of sunscreen washes off swimmers into waterways each year.[24] Does all that washed off product constitute waste? Microplastic fibers from synthetic clothing break off during washing and are accumulating in oceans and in the cells of marine life.[25] How much "waste" from products we use daily goes unrecognized?

Society's understanding of waste will come into line with the reality that resources, waste, and even products are really all the same thing, just in different forms. Eliminating most of today's conventional waste and recognizing the value of all resources, so that what used to be called waste can be recognized as a valuable input, are important, interim steps. But the problem and the opportunities are much bigger than that. Products themselves are largely waste. To understand why, you need to understand the function of products and the relationship between products and wealth.

3

No One Wants
Your Products

YES, YOU READ that right. Even if your company has millions of customers who are buying your products as fast as you can make them, we believe that no one really wants your products. We're making a very important distinction here between your physical products and the function those products perform. People don't buy products because they really want the products. They buy products because they like what the products do for them. In other words, they want the *benefits* they gain by using the products. Nothing is more important for your business than understanding what fundamental benefits your products deliver and then designing future products to optimize resource performance.

> **PEOPLE BUY PRODUCTS BECAUSE THEY LIKE WHAT THE PRODUCTS DO FOR THEM**

What Customers Really Want

Henry Ford famously said, "If I'd asked customers what they wanted, they would have said, 'a faster horse.'" Ford felt that his customers didn't necessarily know what they wanted or that they couldn't imagine the possibilities his company could offer them

Henry Ford said, "If I'd asked customers what they wanted, they would have said, 'a faster horse.'"

through innovation. But Ford sold his customers short. If he had asked *why* they used horses, or what *function* the horses served, or what *benefits* people received by using horses, he would've found that his customers really did know what they wanted.

Here's a short list of what customers *don't* want: light bulbs, refrigerators, washing machines, batteries, DVDs, or books. Here's what they *do* want: light, safe food storage, clean clothes, portable energy that allows them to communicate, listen to music, or find their way safely through the dark, and stories that inform and entertain.

Ford's customers didn't want horses *or* cars. They wanted a safe, quick, affordable, convenient way to transport themselves, other people, and their stuff.

The point is that customers pay for *benefits*. No matter how much a company spends on advertising to make customers feel attached to a particular product, when another company offers a better way to gain the same benefit, people will take it. In the 21st century, it's a mistake for companies to operate on the assumption that customers are paying for the physical stuff, or that they want physical things that we've become accustomed to associating with certain functions. Companies that do will eventually fail, as more and more products are stripped of their physical elements or completely supplanted by entirely new ways of delivering benefits.

Stop and Try This!

Are products verbs or nouns? Can you define products by what they do rather than by their physical forms? For example, a washing machine cleans clothes, a refrigerator stores food safely, insulation maintains temperature.

Choose 10 products related to your business. List the products in column one (as nouns) and redefine them in column two (as verbs).

When you're done, review your redefinitions. Does describing these products by what they do change the way you think about them?

Nouns	Verbs

The Relationship Between Wealth and Resources

There is a relationship between wealth and material resources, but it's a conditional relationship. Under some conditions, more is better. That is, under some conditions, it takes more resources to produce more benefits. But under other conditions, using more resources results in fewer benefits and actually diminishes wealth.

Wealth is more like a capacity than a physical resource. It's about well-being, security, health, and opportunity. Wealth is the ability to do well for a longer time into the future under a wider range of conditions, no matter what goes wrong. People buy products because they perceive that, in some way, having or using those products will contribute to their health or well-being.

Consider a house. It shelters you and your family from storms and other threats; it provides a place to store food and other goods for some time; it has a water supply, a sanitary method to deal with waste, a heat source to keep you warm, and a power source; it includes other amenities that offer various additional benefits. Your house provides safety, security, privacy, and comfort, and it contributes to your family's health.

> **WEALTH IS THE ABILITY TO DO WELL FOR A LONGER TIME INTO THE FUTURE UNDER A WIDER RANGE OF CONDITIONS, NO MATTER WHAT GOES WRONG**

It provides recreational and aesthetic benefits that contribute to your well-being. The house itself isn't your wealth. Wealth stems from the benefits the house provides you. Those benefits don't necessarily have to do with the size of the house or the thickness of its walls. They have to do with your capacity to control your environment, to manage risks, and to meet your needs.

What really matters is the *benefits* people derive from using resources. This concept applies to the economy as a whole, as well as to individuals. In the past, when there were fewer people, vast supplies of easily exploitable resources, and few noticeable environmental impacts, there was a strong correlation between using more resources and producing more benefits (such as a higher standard of living). Under today's conditions, however, using more resources doesn't necessarily result in more benefits. The way to succeed is to produce drastically more benefits with many fewer tons of resources. Many companies are providing successful models, which we describe throughout the remainder of this book.

Products, Resources, and Benefits Today

New scientific and technological advances are making it possible to deliver more benefits to your customers without most of the resources that you think of as essential for your products. To capitalize on these advances, you first

" PRODUCTS AND BENEFITS

ARE NOT THE SAME "

have to answer this key question: What fundamental benefit does your business or product deliver?

Remember, products and benefits are *not* the same. Over time, products have become the symbols of benefits; the two are often

Watch the Video "Value Matters: Innovation Has Direction"

Is a battery manufacturer in the business of producing batteries or selling portable energy? In this five-minute animated video, Howard Brown explains why it's so important for business leaders to understand what customers really want, how companies can align environmental and business metrics, and how technological advances are enabling businesses to deliver more value by using fewer resources.

Watch the video online at dMASS.net.

linked in people's minds. Yet products don't have intrinsic value to people. Their perceived value is derived from the actual benefits they deliver to people who buy or use them. That's why, from a dMASS perspective, value has to do with the useful, measurable benefits a product delivers to a customer relative to resources used. It has to do with how much something contributes to (or diminishes) wealth. The challenge is to identify the hidden benefits embedded in your products.

Think of products as delivery mechanisms for benefits, much like pills or hypodermic needles. Pills and needles deliver medicine intended to improve or maintain health. Ultimately, it's not the mechanism or even the physical medicine that matters. *Health* is the point. That's the benefit people are seeking. Scientists are working now on methods to incorporate vaccines into food, use nanoparticles to seek and destroy cancer cells while leaving healthy cells untouched, and remotely monitor blood pressure with contact lenses.

Researchers are developing ways to trigger the body's ability to regenerate tissue and bone as an alternative to surgery. What we think of as medical devices, pro-

" TRULY INNOVATIVE CHANGE IN PRODUCT DESIGN COMES FROM ASKING, 'HOW CAN WE DO THIS BETTER?' "

cedures, or even medicines today might not exist in a relatively short time. However, the idea that people want to be healthy, that they want to survive and thrive, won't change. For any business today, the central goal should be figuring out how to deliver the benefits people need in new ways with as little resource mass as possible.

It's About Light, Not Light Bulbs

Most people probably think of Thomas Edison as the inventor of a product, the light bulb. But Edison's goal wasn't to create a light bulb. He was interested in figuring out how to harness electricity to provide light. Over time, Edison's incandescent light bulb became synonymous with electric light. Everyone who wanted light bought light bulbs. But really, no one wants light bulbs. Light bulbs are a tool for delivering light where and when it's needed for safety, for performing surgery or studying at night, for illuminating spaces where there's no natural light, and for much more. A light bulb has value only because it can deliver light when and where people need it.

Today, the major challenge for lighting engineers and designers is figuring out how to deliver the naked value of light. This doesn't necessarily mean making a more energy efficient light bulb, or any light bulb at all. Daylighting experts are using fiber optic materials to move natural daylight to the interior sections of buildings where there are no windows, bringing light to where it's needed without using electricity. There's also a shift away from point source bulbs and lamps toward LED sheets, panels, films, strips, and walls. Carbon nanotube technology is enabling the production of thinner, more efficient panels. Designers are incorporating lighting into building infrastructure and aesthetic elements. Two radical examples involve integrating tiny organic light-emitting diode (OLED) granules into wallpaper and into paint to create light-emitting walls. These types of innovations have the potential to not only do away with light bulbs, but with the entire lighting infrastructure in buildings, including fixtures and ballasts. These changes could eliminate much of the resource mass normally tied up in lighting infrastructure, while delivering better, more functional lighting where it's needed.[26]

Truly innovative change in product design doesn't come about by someone asking, "How can we make this thing better?" Instead, it comes from asking, "How can we *do* this better?" In other words, focus on the function, or the desired outcome, not on the material product itself. Ultimately, the goal must be to eliminate nearly all of the material object altogether or to reduce it to its naked value.

Consider this simple example. While many people appreciate the benefits of electronic touchscreen devices such as iPads that don't require keyboards, some of us still miss the feel of a traditional keyboard. We make more typing errors because handling a touchscreen doesn't provide the same feedback as pressing separate keys on a keyboard. What would you do to solve this problem? One option is to design a new portable keyboard. Another, better option is to figure out how to deliver the benefits of a keyboard without any additional resource mass. That's what Chris Harrison, a graduate student at Carnegie Mellon University, did. He developed an ingenious way to deliver the benefits of a keyboard without the keyboard. His invention, the Tesla Touch, employs variable static electricity to trick users' brains and the nerves on their fingers into thinking they're pressing keys on a mechanical keyboard as they operate a touchscreen.[27] Harrison demonstrated that it's possible to re-create the experience of mass without the mass. And he did this by thinking about how to deliver the benefits people wanted, not how to make the material thing more efficient.

Customers are becoming savvier about the relationship between resources, products, and benefits. They want portable energy, but they don't really want to buy and carry disposable batteries. They want to type quickly and accurately, but they don't want to carry a keyboard. They want clean clothes, but don't want to use and pay for the water that makes up a significant portion of most liquid laundry detergents or that's required by today's standard washing machines. When new products come on the market that deliver needed benefits without the invested resources and without as many negative by-products, customers are likely to switch.

Customers want the benefits of products.

Scientific discoveries and technological developments are making it easier for companies to do just that, to bring new products to market that deliver specific benefits customers want while using fewer tons of resources and generating fewer by-products. You don't need to wait for some unknown, futuristic innovation to improve resource performance. For many companies, the process is already under way.

Businesses Focusing on Benefits

Several major companies are succeeding by pursuing a strategy that's more clearly focused on defining and delivering benefits than on selling their traditional products and services. Xerox, for example, once defined itself by the physical products it manufactured and sold, like copiers and printers. Xerox CEO Ursula Burns now says the company helps its customers "transform very complex and burdensome business processes."[28] In other words, though the company still manufactures products, it approaches its business more from the perspective of a service company. It's operating on the premise that its customers want the function or benefits of its products, not necessarily the products themselves. Xerox advises its clients on how to save money in printing costs, even helping clients reduce the number of printing machines and copies they use.[29] The company is also developing an "inkless printer." This printer would use a new type of paper that could be reused (written on and erased multiple times) simply by applying light of a certain wavelength to it, eliminating the need for ink and reducing paper use.[30]

Amazon has a similar approach. CEO Jeff Bezos understands that his company will not succeed just by making and selling better devices. He sees the Kindle Fire as a delivery device for specific services.[31] Bezos argues that companies that focus merely on manufacturing devices will not be successful. He believes that companies should think about the experience customers want and how devices can be leveraged to help deliver that experience.

Waste Management Inc. is in a different industry, but its approach is similar to that of Xerox's and Amazon's. Waste Management found that an increasing number of its clients were expressing interest in zero waste, something that could threaten its core business. The company responded by offering services to help clients achieve zero waste status at their facilities. It embraces the idea that waste is valuable and is shifting its business model to take advantage of new opportunities, even if that means selling less of its traditional product.[32,33]

The movements by Xerox, Amazon, and other companies are intentional. Their actions show that the distinction between physical products and the benefits of those products is an extremely important one. They also reflect a larger, ongoing trend in innovation of devising strategies that deliver more benefits with fewer tons of resources.

4

Innovation Has Direction

INNOVATION ISN'T RANDOM. There's an overarching pattern to discovery. The factors determining the direction of innovation are the same factors that we've already discussed: population growth and resource demands, the increasingly constrained system in which businesses operate, the fact that wastes are actually valuable lost resources, and new discoveries that are making it easier to design resources out of products. Understanding the direction of innovation is an essential step in changing your business and your products to focus more directly on delivering benefits with fewer resources.

> ❝ HUMANITY'S PROGRESSIVE ABILITY TO *DO BETTER WITH LESS*, TO GENERATE MORE WEALTH-PRODUCING BENEFITS FOR MORE PEOPLE WITH FEWER RESOURCES, IS THE LARGEST UNDERLYING TREND IN INNOVATION ❞

Doing Better with Less

Humanity's progressive ability to *do better with less*, to generate more wealth-producing benefits for more people with fewer resources, is the largest underlying trend in innovation and it's the key to creating a sustainable future. This growing ability to do better with less is often associated with certain industries, like information technology. We all know that laptops are capable of doing the work of an old room-sized mainframe. Better with less is a much bigger and more important trend with a long history.

The direction of innovation toward delivering more benefits with fewer resources is visibly evident in bridge design, for example. From the first arch that started as a small hole punched out of a pile of stones, to modern single-wire suspension bridges that span miles, and to future bridges that might be held up by nanowires so thin they're invisible, the evolution of bridge design provides insight into the coming economic and technological revolution.

Bridges are tools for creating wealth. People have used bridges as tools to access resources, to trade with others, and to enable migration for millennia. Over time, people designed and constructed longer and stronger bridges that required fewer tons of material resources per unit of distance spanned or per unit of strength. In other words, people have been designing bridges that deliver more benefits with fewer resources.

You can see this same type of innovation in almost every industry. In aerospace, for example, airplane design is about

Watch the Video "Design Matters: Doing Better with Less"

This short but powerful animated video demonstrates the importance of design for creating sustainable wealth. Using a Buckminster Fuller story as a jumping-off point, Howard Brown explains why the key to successful business strategy today is producing drastically more benefits using drastically fewer resources.

Watch the video online at dMASS.net.

optimizing performance to carry the biggest payload the farthest, fastest, and safest using the fewest possible resources.

Successful Innovation Now

Consider something as simple as the walls of a building. For most of human history, thicker walls meant better insulation, soundproofing, protection from the elements, and protection from invaders. But the challenge here (as in all aspects of any economy) is to figure out how to deliver the benefits of walls with much less resource mass. Researchers, engineers, and builders are increasing the resource performance of walls in several ways, including constructing buildings with thinner materials, finding dual-use applications, and employing phase-change and other adaptable materials. Recent discoveries in materials science are leading to walls that have greater weight-to-strength ratios with longer spans and to buildings with thinner, lighter shells that are stronger and insulate better. Further innovations are expected to result in walls that change color with the touch of a button and without paint, sense and respond to outside conditions, remove unwanted substances from their surfaces, facilitate heating and cooling, serve as lighting elements, heal their own surfaces, generate energy, and break down pollutants.[34]

These aren't just isolated examples or science fiction concepts. dMASS-type innovations are entering the marketplace at an accelerating rate. For instance, Ultra-thin Aerogel is made of the lightest solids known, is strong, breathable, does not absorb water, and is a highly effective insulator. In strips, it can be used to insulate wall studs where there are gaps in insulation in standard wall design.[35] Pythagoras Solar recently introduced photovoltaic window glass that allows solar energy harvesting to be integrated with a building's design.[36] The glass doesn't require any cumbersome, separate structures for holding solar-collecting surfaces.

Some resource performance innovations already in the marketplace are simply lighter re-designs of existing products that deliver more function with less mass. Glass, plastic, and aluminum beverage containers are all becoming thinner, lighter and are using fewer materials (most of which are recycled), while still delivering the same function. Laundry detergent manufacturers introduced two times concentrated liquid detergent, then eight times concentrated, and Tide now sells small laundry detergent "pods" that are highly concentrated and contain very little water. InterfaceFLOR recently introduced a carpet yarn that weighs less and uses less yarn per carpet tile without performance loss.[37] Adidas sells a high-performance running shoe that weighs only about six ounces, compared to a typical training shoe at 12 ounces.[38] There are countless examples of products that are similar to their predecessors, but use relatively straightforward methods to reduce mass while retaining or even enhancing benefits.

> dMASS-TYPE INNOVATIONS ARE ENTERING THE MARKETPLACE AT AN ACCELERATING RATE

Other recent innovations incorporate new methods and technologies that enable much more dramatic resource mass savings and performance improvements. Two innovative manufacturing techniques, *printing* and *growing,* have enormous potential for reducing the amount of mass required for fabrication. Designer and biologist Suzanne Lee is using bacteria to grow microbial-cellulose fiber that she can dry and then shape or sew into a purse

Stop and Try This!

Grab two pens of different colors and some index cards.

Start by thinking about a building envelope, or a building enclosure (the parts of a building that separate the inside of the building from the outside world). Consider all the *functions* or *benefits* you'd expect or would like to have and write each one on a different index card. Examples include structure, weather protection, temperature control, privacy, visibility, aesthetics, and energy generation.

Now think of all the *material parts* of a building envelope you can, including all the different layers of a wall. Using a different color pen, write each of these on a separate card. Examples include framing, or a piece of clothing.[39] The material, which can substitute for leather and for petroleum-derived fabrics, requires much less dye than other fibers and is biodegradable. Lee imagines a world in which we can grow our clothing fully formed, directly from a vat of liquid.

An additive manufacturing technology, 3D printing, holds great potential for reducing the tons of material resources used in

vapor barriers, insulation, siding, paint, plywood, drywall, windows, wall coverings, and solar panels.

Spread all the cards out on a table. How could you combine these things? How could you combine different material parts? How could you alter the parts so they deliver multiple benefits? How could you change the relationship between benefits and materials to eliminate mass?

Now try the above exercise with something related to your business. Practice thinking about the relationship between benefits and resource mass and the possibilities for delivering more benefits with fewer resources. Where are the opportunities to deliver something more effectively, yet save money and resources? The more you do this, the more opportunities you will see around you.

products. 3D printing refers to a technology that works much like a desktop printer, but it prints finished products. Instead of ink, a 3D printer uses a carefully calculated and measured combination of basic elements that bond together as they are laid down, layer by layer. There is very little scrap because the molecular formations comprising the outcome are added so precisely that the product appears in the exact shape desired. Moreover, because the equipment for 3D printing itself is becoming smaller, lighter, and less expensive, it will enable manufacturing to move back closer to users, which can reduce total life-cycle resource use. Manufacturers have used 3D printing for rapid prototyping for some time, but the technology has advanced enough that it's becoming more viable for production. General Electric is testing 3D printing for jet engine parts to save weight, fuel, and materials. The company plans to undertake a "major weight-reduction scavenger hunt," searching for parts that can be streamlined with the aid of 3D printing.[40]

Nanotechnology is another important field. In nanomedicine, researchers are developing solutions for targeted drug delivery.[41] New medicines are designed to affect only cancer cells, for example, while leaving healthy cells unharmed. This kind of strategy could reduce the amount of drugs manufactured and ingested, and also reduce harmful side effects. There are nanotechnology solutions in development in every field for everything from high-performing fabrics to better large-scale energy storage and more effective energy harvesting.

Finally, biomimicry holds considerable promise for helping to deliver more benefits with fewer resources. There are countless examples of natural processes that accomplish amazing things without high temperatures, toxic chemicals, heavy structures, or large inputs of energy. Scientists, designers, and architects are using nature as a model to solve problems in many different settings.

As technology enables new forms, designs, and solutions, companies need to continuously realign what they offer with the benefits customers need. If you aim for naked value, consistent with the direction of innovation, you might not achieve it overnight, but you will come out ahead by working toward this goal. Each improvement in energy efficiency, recycling, purchasing, packaging reduction, and so forth needs to be understood as an incremental step in eliminating mass in your entire customer value delivery process.

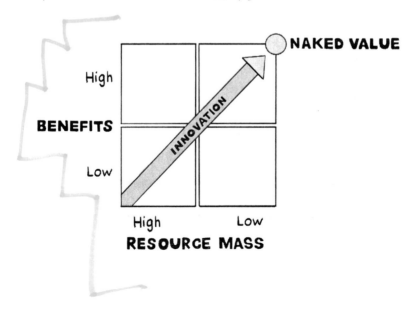

Remember the figure from the introduction, which shows the direction of innovation toward naked value? It's a reminder to strip away resources from your business and from your products in pursuit of naked value. Your products will likely look different. You might even put yourself out of the business you think you're in today. But you will discover how to deliver the benefits your customers want with the fewest possible resources. Every action that improves the relationship between resources used and benefits delivered represents progress for your business. You can be sure that there are competitors out there right now developing solutions that deliver more benefits with fewer resources in entirely new ways.

5

You Don't Know
Your Competition

THE BIGGEST THREAT TO your business probably won't be the result of another company's incremental product improvement. It will result from drastic resource reductions in a product, its packaging, and its entire supply chain. Or this threat will be an entirely new product that performs the same function as yours (maybe even better than yours does) but doesn't resemble your product at all. It might already be in some stage of development in a research lab or at a start-up company.

Your biggest threat will come from a company whose leaders recognize that the business is about delivering benefits, not stuff. It might originate from the other side of the globe or from an unrecognized competitor down the street, a start-up based on scientific research emerging from a university lab, or an existing company that operates in an entirely different field. It probably won't come from your traditional competitors.

Disruption Is Already Happening

Some stories about industries turned upside down in recent years are probably familiar to you. Not long ago, music-recording companies were thriving, as were companies that sold records, tapes, CDs, and music players. Together, these companies controlled the music supply chain, from identifying and selecting talent to recording, marketing, and distributing products. The leaders of once-giant record companies like Capitol and Columbia no doubt thought they were primarily competing against each other. They didn't foresee the implications of a rapid shift to digital media. When low-cost digital recording met the Internet, new markets and marketing channels emerged. Suddenly, musicians didn't need the recording companies to "discover" them or to produce their music. Then, tiny digital music players further disrupted production and sales.[42] Music distribution went weightless. Now even these music players are marching toward obsolescence because mobile phones incorporate the miniscule circuits needed to decode digital data.

Today, the wireless communication of digital music is replacing the physical mass of CDs, as well as the warehouses needed to store CDs, the trucks needed to distribute them, and the retail shelf space needed to display them. These changes did not come about through traditional industry competitors. They came from companies that didn't even exist a decade earlier, like Facebook and YouTube, and from tech companies like Apple, which introduced the iPod in 2000. The products from these companies didn't look anything like the record companies' products.

Similar stories are playing out in every industry. In carpeting, InterfaceFLOR developed a new way to keep commercial carpet in place, replacing the need for huge quantities of toxic adhesives. Their solution—an application of biomimicry—is based on reproducing the adhesive properties of geckos' feet (the properties that allow the animals to walk on walls and ceilings). A two-pound roll of Interface's tiny sticky tiles, which are placed only at the corners of carpet squares, provides as much function as a 42-pound bucket of glue.[43] The makers of carpet adhesive probably thought that their competitors were other adhesive companies offering similar adhesive products. Now there's a competitor offering an entirely different solution. Their product innovation looks different and

Where will your competition come from?

requires far fewer resource inputs, from the resources embedded in the product itself to resources related to mining, manufacturing, shipping, and warehousing. Plus, the new adhesive solution doesn't require additional toxic chemicals to remove it when the carpet reaches the end of its useful life, nor does it interfere with the recycling of carpet fibers. Pollution and waste throughout the product's entire life cycle are drastically lower and an entire product category is at risk of becoming obsolete.

It's Just the Beginning

Fueled by growing scientific knowledge and emerging technologies, many more disruptive products are in the works. General Electric is developing water-repellant metals by altering the metals' surface so that water beads up and rolls off. If they can translate this technology to airplane wings, ice would not be able to form on the wings.[44] This could mean the elimination of an entire industry of deicing chemicals, along with the trucks and energy used in the deicing process, the contaminated runoff at airports, take-off delays, and fuel burned during delays. Again, companies manufacturing deicing chemicals are likely focused on competition from one another and on modifying their existing processes, not on a new approach that eliminates the need for deicing altogether and uses a fraction of the resources.

New technologies are also in development in the fabrics industry. For example, there are new methods that eliminate the need for waterproofing treatments and for cleaning agents. A fabric with tiny spikes on its surface at the nano-level repels water so that the fabric can't become wet and is self-cleaning.[45] A scientist is working on a molecular technology to color fabric without dye.[46]

Every indication is that this trend will continue in virtually every industry and in every market sector. The changes are not just in technology, but also in the manner businesses are organized to deliver technology.

Disruptive Business Models

Disruptive business models might not seem similar to the technology-enabled changes in products from various industries, but they are absolutely part of the same trend of increasing resource performance. For example, sharing and collaborative consumption are dMASS strategies that are about enhancing resource performance through the way that products are used. They involve taking resources already in circulation, increasing the intensity of use for those resources or capturing their idle capacity, and harvesting more wealth-producing benefits from them. Collaborative consumption advocate Rachel Botsman points out that the average power drill is used for only about 12 minutes in its lifetime.[47] Sharing strategies aim to increase resource performance by delivering the benefit people need (in this case, a hole) with a fraction of the resources required by the ubiquitous ownership of drills.

Business models are emerging around the more effective

utilization of resources in everything from tools to consumer goods, capital, land, building surface areas, transportation vehicles, and various kinds of equipment. In some places, it's now possible to rent a luxury handbag, borrow a car or a bike, rent land for gardening, lease a rooftop for solar applications, [48] or use a spare desk in an office. [49] Many sharing activities aren't new, but they're expanding in novel ways due to an increased recognition of resources' value, and they are being facilitated by technology that helps people with common interests readily find one another. The result is a reduction in processed, valuable resources sitting idle. Instead, these resources are engaged in providing more benefits to more people. Businesses and individuals also have more opportunities to purchase benefits, because collaborative consumption costs are lower than the costs of ownership.

Zip Car is one prominent business based on a sharing model. With the high cost of car ownership, including insurance, maintenance, and parking, it often makes financial sense to share. Despite continued population growth, there's evidence that the developed world has reached "peak" car ownership. [50] In both the United States and the United Kingdom, per capita driving miles have decreased, and the portion of young people with a driver's license is less than in previous generations. There are many factors at play here, including economic conditions and the availability of public transportation, but there also seems to be a cultural shift away from the ownership of many different kinds of goods.

(The collaborative economy)

Business models designed to increase resource performance aren't limited to sharing. For example, small manufacturer Thogus Products has been suggested as a possible model for the future of manufacturing. According to the company's CEO, "I don't consider us a manufacturing company anymore. We're a technology and services company."[51] The company employs engineers, provides input on product design, and produces customized goods. The Thogus approach fits into a future that isn't simply about manufacturing products but is also about providing services that customers can use to tailor products that use fewer resources and deliver more precisely targeted benefits.

> THE QUESTION 'WHAT ARE MY COMPETITORS DOING?' HAS LESS RELEVANCE THAN EVER

The Knockout Competition

As a business leader, it's essential for you to discard old assumptions about competition. The question "what are my competitors doing?" has less relevance than ever. Given that customers really want the benefits of products and that innovation is about progressively delivering more of those benefits with fewer resources, your competition probably isn't where you think it is. Tomorrow's potential knockout competition will arise because someone figures out how to deliver what you're delivering with far fewer resources. To compete, you need to look at your own products in a different way.

6

Your Products Are
Mostly Waste

How CAN YOU deliver naked value? Instead of making more, you can rearrange less.

Every business imports material resources from our environment and rearranges those resources into products to create wealth. The key word here is *rearrange*. Among the millions of manufacturing firms around the world, none of them actually *make* things in the sense that they don't add any energy or materials to the universe.

There's a corollary on the customers' side: Among the billions of people in the world, none of them *consume* anything. In this new business environment, it will be harder and harder to operate a successful business if you think that you make things and that customers consume them. Customers purchase resources that are organized into products, and they use those resources as long as the resources provide a desired benefit. Then they either return those resources back to the environment at the end of a product's useful life or back into the economy for reuse and recycling. Customers don't consume anything.

The Real Meaning of Waste

Customers really want wealth, not waste. As we stated earlier, waste is much more than what gets lost from a manufacturing process, trucked to a landfill, released through a smokestack, or washed into a wastewater stream. Waste is all resources brought into the industrial economy and converted from one form to another that yield little or no wealth-enhancing benefits. It includes all the resources used by a company and its suppliers that aren't essential to delivering benefits to customers—including materials in your products.

> **WASTE INCLUDES ALL THE RESOURCES USED BY A COMPANY AND ITS SUPPLIERS THAT AREN'T ESSENTIAL TO DELIVERING BENEFITS**

Much of what companies sell provides little or no value. Sunscreen washes away in the water when people swim. Toothpaste goes down the drain. Excess packaging goes straight into the trash. Many products are largely composed of water, bulking agents, and other ingredients that make the products feel substantial or protect shelf space but deliver little or no additional benefits to customers. Products break or become obsolete while their embedded resources remain tied up, unavailable for reinvestment to produce more wealth. Resource recovery and recycling are essential parts of improving resource performance, but they are not adequate. Extracting more value from resources by recycling products requires expending more energy and resource capital.

How many resources are required to deliver a product's benefit?

Stop and Try This!

Take some time to think about how you can move a product closer to naked value. Look at the chart and consider the relative position of product categories A-D. Use the list below to help you identify potential incremental resource improvements:

(A) Identify the baseline benefits and resource mass of your product. Create a very simple description of what your product provides to customers and then jot down a list of the major resource inputs for the product.

(B) How could you reduce the product's resource inputs while retaining benefits?

(C) How could you increase benefits while keeping resource inputs the same?

(D) Identify potential strategies that reduce mass *and* increase benefits.

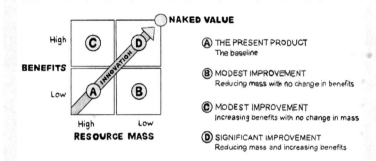

Figure 3: Improving Resource Performance

Now use the product categories A-D to describe what your product might look like with different performance improvements, and describe your product in its naked value form. For example, if your company manufactures toothpaste (providing a dental health benefit), the baseline is toothpaste. A product with the same benefits and decreased mass might be a cleaning agent that comes in a thin strip form. A naked value product might be a semipermanent "paint" that protects teeth from bacteria, tartar, and decay for months at a time. Can you think of new ways to deliver more benefits with fewer resources?

Though waste minimization has been an important element in corporate environmental management for some time, it has had a limited scope. It has been re-

RESOURCES AND BENEFITS ARE THE TWO MOST IMPORTANT CONCEPTS FOR BUSINESSES TODAY

stricted mainly to scrap, or the leftovers and obvious excesses of manufacturing. When you consider a more expansive view of waste, you can begin to see new ways to eliminate waste and costs by rethinking the very nature of your products.

When waste is defined as everything that's not needed to deliver value to customers, zero waste takes on a new meaning. Eliminating waste becomes a continuous process of removing material resources from every part of your business, even from your products. It involves a willingness to reorient your thinking about what business you're in and what your products are.

Rearrange Less, Deliver More

You should know how much benefit every one of your products delivers and the quantity of resources you are investing in those products. Only then can you figure out how to deliver the benefits your customers need with the fewest resources and by-products possible.

Your company pays for every ton of resource mass associated with your business, including the ones that add benefit, the ones that are lost to pollution or waste while they're in your company's hands, and the ones that your customers throw away. The goal is to rearrange fewer resources while delivering more benefits.

So, resources and benefits are the two most important concepts for businesses today. Doing better with less is about continuously improving the relationship between resources used and benefits delivered, which means improving resource performance. Value increases with resource performance improvements that:

- Increase benefits and reduce resource mass
- Maintain benefits and reduce resource mass
- Increase benefits and maintain resource mass

Putting It All Together: Steps Toward Achieving Naked Value

Now that we've identified the six critical concepts needed to succeed in a resource-constrained world, let's look at how to use this knowledge to reduce costs and risks, gain competitive advantage in your markets, and breathe new excitement into your business. After all, the goal is to advance your business.

The dMASS Approach

There are two methods for implementing a dMASS approach to achieving naked value. One uses your existing product as a starting point. It includes a series of steps to guide you through incremental resource performance improvements. The other focuses on designing a disruptive solution that delivers benefits in a new way. It's important to understand both so you can determine which of these approaches is most appropriate for your company. Both methods have the same eventual outcome: a product with naked value. Some companies opt to use the methods simultaneously.

Before we look at specific methods, let's review a few simple principles. Every business needs to understand and measure the total amount of resources used for each product. That total resource quantity, measured as mass (weight) is the product's resource footprint. It's not only essential for calculating and measuring costs and for improving your competitive advantage in the marketplace, it's an indicator of a variety of risks ranging from resource supply and price vulnerability to environmental impacts.

Given a static amount of resources invested in each product, an increase in sales volume means increased demand for energy, water, and materials. As sales increase, your company might buy more manufacturing machinery, parts, and packaging from suppliers. These suppliers, in turn, will need more materials from their suppliers. All of this activity will result in more fuel use, more water use, and so on. A resource demand multiplier effect ripples through the supply chain.

Similarly, a dMASS multiplier occurs with resource savings. When your company reduces the resources in each product, resource savings ripple back through the supply chain. Every reduction in product mass results in decreased demand for energy, materials, and water at each step in the supply chain. With a significant resource reduction, your company can even increase sales while decreasing resource use. As we have discussed, that can mean lower costs, higher profits, less environmental risk, and a better competitive market position.

Understanding and even reducing resource use isn't enough to navigate global competition, radical new technologies, and changing public interest in what makes products desirable. It's easy to reduce resource use in ways that also reduce the quality, durability, or usefulness of the product, or increase its toxicity, and that won't do. In fact, reducing resources used in a product without adequate consideration of its impact on product value can actually cause total resource use to grow elsewhere as people seek other ways to meet their needs.

Every business leader needs to be able to measure the essential, primal benefits delivered to customers by each product or service. Only by knowing the relationship between the essential benefits delivered and the quantity of resources required to deliver them can businesses act methodically to innovate, gain competitive advantage, and achieve naked value. To do that, you need to regularly monitor the changes in the benefits your products deliver, as

$$\text{Change in Performance} = \frac{\text{Change in Benefits}}{\text{Change in Resource Mass}}$$

An increase in performance comes about by either increasing benefits or reducing resource mass or both.

well as changes in the quantity of resources needed to deliver those
benefits.

The Step-by-Step Method: Uncovering Your Product's Naked Value

If you plan to achieve naked value through incremental resource
performance improvements of an existing product, start with the
process below. There are countless business tools designed to help
companies make strategic decisions with information on competitors and customers, market conditions, and value chains. These
tools are useful, but don't necessarily lead to the sort of innovation that companies require to thrive. Our process will guide you
through specific questions related to resource performance. The
text and accompanying diagram describe each step.

Note that this is an iterative process designed to support
continuous improvement. What you learn from the later steps will
inform and refine your understanding of the first steps. It will be
most effective if you repeat the process, expanding the detail of
analysis with each iteration.

Step 1: Define Your Product's Naked Value. Your first step is
to define your goal, your product's naked value. What *benefits* do
the material components of the product deliver?

This isn't easy; we all identify with the physical products we
use and make. Remember that benefits and the familiar products
that deliver them are not the same thing. So think about *why* your

customers buy your product. What benefits do they gain by using your product? Continue to ask these questions again and again until you arrive at the most fundamental aspect of your product, its weightless and invisible essence. This essence is your product's naked value, which will be the central focus of your product redesign and the key to measuring your progress.

Step 2: Make It Measurable. Identifying your product's naked value is extremely important, but it's not enough. Translating this way of thinking about your product into a successful dMASS design innovation requires making the product's value measurable. Therefore, the second step in this process is to modify your definition of naked value so that it's in measurable terms.

For example, if your product is toothpaste and you defined its naked value as oral hygiene, now you need to add a unit of measure, such as volume, time, or energy. In this case, it makes sense to use something like the number of days of oral hygiene that the product provides customers. So, if using a certain quantity of toothpaste results in one day of oral hygiene and there is enough for 30 uses in one tube, that tube equals 30 days of oral hygiene for your customers. In some cases, there might be more than one measure, but start with the primary benefit and then you can define secondary benefits later.

Having a measurable benefit allows you to establish a resource performance baseline, to create a benchmark with industry standards or with specific competitors, and, most important, to plot your progressive improvements in resource performance over time. Later, it will help you identify opportunities for reducing mass. If you can't quantify progress based on the product's benefits more precisely than units sold or dollars in revenue, then you need to return to the first step and rework your definition of naked value.

Step 3: Calculate Invested Mass. The next step is to document the total amount of mass tied up in your product. This must include all resources, from fuels to metals, plastics, minerals, earth aggregates, and water. List all the components and raw materials used in the manufacture and delivery of your product and assemble an inventory of all resources used by weight and by process. If your company has recently conducted a life cycle assessment, that assessment will contain a great deal of the resource data you need for this mass calculation.

The first calculation will be your product's baseline. Because resource performance improvement is an iterative process, you'll need to recalculate the mass with each design change to evaluate progress. It's okay to start out with a simple calculation based on easily accessible information and then create a more detailed calculation in the next round. With each calculation, you can use the results to evaluate strategies, designs, and tactical business decisions.

Step 4: Define the Problem. A problem is the difference between the way things are and the way you want them to be. In terms of resource performance, the way things are is the amount of mass currently tied up in your product relative to the amount of benefits your product delivers. That's your baseline. The way you want things to be is the measurable naked value as you defined it in steps one and two, delivered with minimal mass.

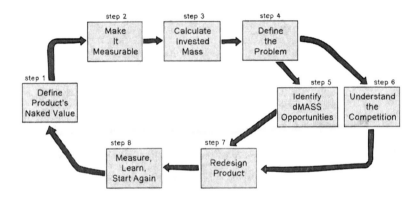

Figure 4: Step-by-Step to Naked Value

Achieving naked value through incremental resource performance improvements.

Step 5: Identify Opportunities to Improve Resource Performance. Now you need to find and eliminate mass embodied in your product, your manufacturing, and your distribution processes that is not actually essential for delivering naked value. It takes time to really understand how you currently use resources to deliver benefits. Spend some time identifying potential opportunities to increase resource performance. Assemble an inventory of ideas. Then prioritize the inventory by potential impact (resource reductions and benefit increases), cost, and difficulty of implementation.

Step 6: Understand Your Competition. While you're looking at ways to deliver more benefits with fewer resources, so are your competitors. Remember that your greatest threats will probably not come from your present competition. You need to be aware of the new science, technologies, and business models that can be leveraged to improve resource performance. You don't need to understand the science precisely, but you need to be aware that technologies and scientific discoveries are emerging quickly and that the realm of what's possible is changing.

To identify potential competitors who could disrupt your industry and/or product, think in terms of benefits delivered rather than physical products. Can you identify a product or service in a completely different sector that could deliver the same or similar benefits to customers with fewer resources than your product uses? Are emerging technologies in your domain or in another industry threatening your product's survival?

One risk many businesses create for themselves is the tendency to avoid new investments and opportunities and to stay with a cash cow, thinking it's safe, even when new technologies begin to emerge in the marketplace. It's important to invest in alternatives that deliver more benefits with fewer resources, especially if your company's chief product is stagnant or losing market share.

Step 7: Redesign Your Product. Imagine your ideal product as one that delivers benefits to your customers with the absolute minimum amount of resources, including all materials, fuels, and water. That must become your goal. Every business decision you make should involve consideration of how it will help you achieve naked value. You need to be bold in your thinking.

The changes you make in pursuit of naked value might not always be visible in your product redesigns, but they will be visible in the operational cost structure and resource mass required to manufacture and deliver the product. Consider each small change as a step toward your goal of naked value.

Step 8: Measure, Learn, and Start Again. Resource performance is a continuous improvement process that's never finished. With each step, you learn more, identify more opportunities, and get better.

Moreover, as you implement resource performance improvements, you need to create an ever-widening circle of coworkers at all levels to participate in and improve the process. Ultimately, the process needs to involve top management (including the CEO and CFO), as well as marketing, product design, manufacturing, purchasing, environment, and sustainability professionals, to name a few.

The Disruptive Method: Designing a New Product with Naked Value

Imagine a product that is nothing more than a pattern. A pattern that can deliver benefits, replace the need to use tons of resources, and eliminate tons of waste.

A weightless pattern, invisible to the naked eye, is the basis of the products from biotech company Sharklet Technologies.[52] The Sharklet idea was developed for ship hulls, but now it has the potential to disrupt an entirely different industry. When we learned about Sharklet while researching this book, we realized that it's an excellent example of a disruptive product brought about by asking the right questions about the benefits customers need, rather than through incremental improvements in an existing product.

To understand how the Sharklet technology works, you need some background. Algae grows on the surface of ships and submarines. It interferes with mechanical functions, attracts other metal-corroding organisms, and increases drag, which increases fuel consumption. The traditional method for fighting algae growth is to apply tons of antifouling toxic chemicals and paints, which requires expensive and time-consuming dry-docking and produces harmful by-products. This costly resource-intensive method was ripe for a dMASS-type solution.

Dr. Anthony Brennan, a professor of materials science and engineering, came up with a solution while working on a project for the U.S. Office of Naval Research. He discovered that a microscopic pattern on the surface of sharkskin inhibits algae growth. He realized that incorporating this pattern into the surface of ship hulls could deliver the benefits the navy wanted—clean ship hulls —while saving materials, time, maintenance costs, and fuel, and reducing environmental risks.

He and his colleagues also figured out that the sharkskin pattern could be used to create bacteria-resistant surfaces. Harmful bacteria grow on all kinds of surfaces, including hospital equipment and kitchen counters. The typical method for combatting these bacteria is to use tons of chemicals to kill them, which is resource-intensive, and costly and is contributing to the rise of antibiotic-resistant superbugs. Sharklet Technologies produces thin films with the sharkskin pattern, which can be applied to surfaces to inhibit the spread of dangerous bacteria. It also produces medical equipment with the sharkskin pattern built into their surfaces. The pattern provides bacteria resistance without adding any additional mass.

In the case of combatting either algae growth or bacteria growth, a company could have pursued incremental improvements, such as making the chemicals stronger, reducing the chemicals' packaging, or developing a similar but less toxic formula. Instead, the people behind Sharklet focused on benefits customers want. The navy doesn't want antifouling chemicals; it wants clean ship hulls. Hospitals don't want tons of antibacterial chemicals; they want to minimize the risk of complications caused by the spread of harmful bacteria. Sharklet Technologies' solution has the potential to eliminate toxic products and to save tons of material resources.

The sharkskin pattern demonstrates how products themselves can be waste. It shows how an industry might be blindsided by completely unknown competition working in a different field. And it illustrates how innovation continues to move in one direction: toward naked value.

Thousands of similar innovation stories are emerging all over the world, in new companies and in established ones with mature products. You can find them within your own business processes, and you can find them in your customers' lives and businesses. Whether you begin with small incremental steps for your existing products or go right for the bold disruptive design, the key to success is *intentional* and *systematic* progress toward achieving naked value.

> " INNOVATION CONTINUES TO MOVE IN ONE DIRECTION: TOWARD NAKED VALUE "

Notes

Note: All online articles were reaccessed in April 2012. "Unknown" is used when the physical location of the publishing entity was unavailable.

1. Throughout the remainder of the book, we refer to products and services simply as products. Resource use associated with material products is obvious – at least the portion of the resources that wind up in the products themselves. But dMASS is not just about reducing the resource mass in products and packaging. It's about the entire supply chain. Service delivery requires resource use too, so service providers need to develop dMASS plans. Consider the fuels, water, and materials used for office space, vehicle use, computers, storage facilities, and so on. Like products, services can benefit from resource performance improvements.

2. Thomas Reuters. "The World at 7 Billion – Growing Population." *The Knowledge Effect.* http://blog.thomsonreuters.com/

index.php/the-world-at-7-billion-growing-population/.

3. For example, energy intensity (the energy required to produce a unit of GDP, or gross domestic product) is declining across most of the globe. One prediction is that differences in energy intensity between nations will even out by 2030. See *The Economist* online. "Energy Use: Power Slide," January 19, 2011. *The Economist*. http://www.economist.com/blogs/dailychart/2011/01/energy_use?fsrc=scn/tw/te/dc/powerslide.

4. Lee, Mike. "Water Worries Span the Globe." *The San Diego Union-Tribune*, September 19, 2011. http://www.utsandiego.com/news/2011/sep/19/water-worries-span-globe/.

5. *The Guardian* (London), "The Six Natural Resources Most Drained by Our 7 billion People," October 31, 2011. http://www.guardian.co.uk/environment/blog/2011/oct/31/six-natural-resources-population.

6. Fischer-Kowalski, M., Swilling, M., von Weizsäcker, E.U., Ren, Y., Moriguchi, Y., Crane, W., Krausmann, F., Eisenmenger, N., Giljum, S., Hennicke, P., Romero Lankao, P., Siriban Manalang, A., Sewerin, S. *Decoupling Natural Resource Use and Environmental Impacts from Economic Growth:*

A Report of the Working Group on Decoupling to the International Resource Panel. Online: United Nations Environment Programme, 2011. http://www.unep.org/resourcepanel/decoupling/files/pdf/decoupling_report_english.pdf.

7. "Risk List 2011." British Geological Survey (BGS). http://www.bgs.ac.uk/mineralsuk/statistics/riskList.html.

8. Haxel, Gordon B., James B. Hedrick, and Greta J. Orris. "Rare Earth Elements — Critical Resources for High Technology: USGS Fact Sheet 087-02." USGS Publications Warehouse. http://pubs.usgs.gov/fs/2002/fs087-02/.

9. Areddy, James T., David Fickling, and Norihiko Shirouzu. "China Denies Halting Rare-Earth Exports to Japan." *The Wall Street Journal* (New York), September 23, 2010, sec. Asia News. http://online.wsj.com/article/SB1000142405 2748704062804575509640345070222.html?KEYWOR DS=china+minerals#articleTabs%3Darticle.

10. "Water: Keeping Our Economy Flowing." Ceres — Igniting 21st Century Solutions for a Sustainable Economy. http://www.ceres.org/issues/water.

11. Rotella, Carlo. "Can Jeremy Grantham Profit from

Ecological Mayhem?" *The New York Times* (New York), August 11, 2011, sec. Magazine. http://www.nytimes. com/2011/08/14/magazine/can-jeremy-grantham-profit-from-ecological-mayhem.html?pagewanted=all.

12.   Jeremy Grantham's quarterly letters are available through the GMO website: http://www.gmo.com/America/.

13.   Osborn, Jeremy. "Corporate Water Disclosure: The Devil Is in the Details." *The Guardian* (London), January 24, 2011, sec. The Guardian Sustainable Business Water Hub. http:// www.guardian.co.uk/sustainable-business/corporate-water-disclosure-response-disappointing-details?intcmp=239.

14.   Jenkinson, Kirsty, and Joe Rozza. "Aqueduct Sheds New Light on Water Risks for Business." *The Guardian* (London), September 16, 2011, sec. The Guardian Sustainable Business Water Hub. http://www.guardian.co.uk/sustainable-business/aqueduct-water-risks-coca-cola-sustainability and http://insights.wri.org/aqueduct/welcome.

15.   Graham Richard, Michael. "Toyota Is Working on Electric Motors That Don't Require Chinese Rare Earths." *Treehugger* (Unknown), January 18, 2011, sec. Transportation. http:// www.treehugger.com/files/2011/01/toyota-electric-

motor-doesnt-require-china-rare-earth.php.

16. *Greentech Enterprise*, "Toyota, Scientists Spear-
    head Mineral Recycling for EVs," October 29, 2010.
    http://www.greentechmedia.com/articles/read/
    toyota-univ.-tokyo-spearhead-rare-earth-nickel-recycling/.

17. Clifford, Stephanie. "Devilish Packaging, Tamed." *The New
    York Times* (New York), June 1, 2011, sec. Business Day: Ener-
    gy & Environment. http://www.nytimes.com/2011/06/02/
    business/energy-environment/02packaging.
    html?_r=1&partner=rss&emc=rss.

18. Thorpe, Lorna. "InterfaceFLOR — Closing the Loop in the
    Manufacturing Process." *The Guardian* (London), May 26,
    2011, sec. Guardian Sustainable Business Waste & Recycling
    Hub.   http://www.guardian.co.uk/sustainable-business/
    closing-loop-manufacturing-process-reduce-waste.

19. "Zero Waste." InterfaceFLOR. http://www.interfaceflor.
    com/Default.aspx?Section=3&Sub=4&Ter=2.

20. Zero Waste International Alliance defines zero waste as the
    recovery of all resources and elimination of "all discharges
    to land, water or air that are a threat to planetary, human,

animal or plant health." Programs that divert 90 percent or
more of waste away from landfills and incinerators are generally accepted as zero waste. See "About Us." Zero Waste
International Alliance. http://zwia.org/joomla/index.php?.

21. Bardelline, Jonathan. "Half of General Motors' Plants
Achieve Landfill-Free Status." *GreenBiz* (Oakland), December 14, 2010. http://www.greenbiz.com/news/2010/
12/14/half-general-motors-plants-achieve-landfill-free-
status#ixzz1867fFQxO.

22. *Environmental Leader* (Fort Collins), "Sprint Unveils Zero E-
Waste Goal," May 27, 2011. http://www.environmentallead-
er.com/2011/05/27/sprint-unveils-zero-e-waste-goal/.

23. "Drug Disposal — National Take-Back Initiative." DEA
Diversion Control Program. http://www.deadiversion.us-
doj.gov/drug_disposal/takeback/.

24. Goleman, Daniel. *Ecological Intelligence: How Knowing the
Hidden Impacts of What We Buy Can Change Everything.*
New York: Broadway Books, 2009.

25. Kinver, Mark. "Accumulating 'Microplastic' Threat to
Shores." *BBC News* (London), January 27, 2012, sec. Science

& Environme12s Printer." *The Future of Things* (Unknown), February 15, 2007, sec. General Technology. http://thefutureofthings.com/articles/50/xerox-inkless-printer.html.

26. For example, see "Lighting, Labeling and Materials: The Latest dMASS Newsletter," February 11, 2011. http://www.dmass.net/wordpress/index.php/2011/02/11/lighting-labeling-and-materials-the-latest-dmass-newsletter/ and related articles at dMASS.net.

27. "Teslatouch." Disney Research — The Science Behind the Magic. http://www.disneyresearch.com/research/projects/hci_teslatouch_drp.htm/media.html.

28. Anthony, Scott D., and Clayton M. Christensen. "The Empire Strikes Back: How Xerox and Other Big Corporations Are Harnessing the Force of Disruptive Innovation." *MIT Technology Review* (Cambridge), December 1, 2011, sec. Business. http://www.technologyreview.com/business/39205/.

29. Winston, Andrew. "Ask Customers to Use Less of Your Product: The Big Heresy." *Harvard Business Review* (Cambridge), February 10, 2011. http://blogs.hbr.org/winston/2011/02/ask-customers-to-use-less-of-y.html.

30. Genuth, Iddo. "Xerox Inkless Printer." *The Future of Things* (Unknown), February 15, 2007, sec. General Technology. http://thefutureofthings.com/articles/50/xerox-inkless-printer.html.

31. Schonfeld, Erick. "Bezos: 'In The Modern Era Of Consumer Electronics Devices, If You Are Just Building A Device You Are Unlikely To Succeed.' " *TechCrunch* (Unknown), September 29, 2011. http://techcrunch.com/2011/09/29/bezos-in-the-modern-era-of-consumer-electronics-devices-if-you-are-just-building-a-device-you-are-unlikely-to-succeed/.

32. Waste Management. "Sustainability: Think Green Every Day." Waste & Recycling Services for Homes & Businesses — Waste Management. http://www.wm.com/sustainability/index.jsp.

33. Clancy, Heather. "Waste Management: There's Gold in That Municipal Waste." *Smart Planet* (Unknown), February 10, 2011, sec. Business. http://www.smartplanet.com/business/blog/business-brains/waste-management-theres-gold-in-that-municipal-waste/13658/.

34. See, for example, past issues of dMASS newsletters and

Grupe, Robert, and Ryan Kirsch, "When These Walls Can Talk." *Design Intelligence*, January 3, 2011, sec. Articles. http://www.di.net/articles/archive/when_these_walls_can_talk/.

Sandén, Björn, Sverker Molander, Martin Hassellöv, and Hans Fogelberg. "Nanotech in Our Homes — Great Opportunities, Unknown Risks." *Sustainability: Journal from the Swedish Research Council Formas* November (2008). http://sustainability.formas.se/en/Issues/Issue-3/Content/Focus-container/Toxicants-in-combination/.

Stobbs, John. "The Lees Concept of Eco-Skin." *John Stobbs — Reporting* (Unknown), November 12, 2011. http://johnstobbs.blogspot.com/2011/02/lees-concept-of-eco-skin.html.

35. Jetson Green. "Ultra-Thin Super Insulation with Aerogel," February 4, 2010. http://www.jetsongreen.com/2010/02/aerogel-ultra-thin-super-insulation.html.

36. "Home page." Pythagoras Solar. http://pythagoras-solar.com/.

37. *Business Standard* (Mumbai), "InterfaceFLOR Launches Biosfera I: The Industry's Most Sustainable Carpet Tiles,"

June 28, 2011, sec. Announcement/Corporate. http://www.
business-standard.com/india/news/interfaceflor-launches-
biosfera-iindustrys-most-sustainable-carpet-tiles/440891/.

38. Fraioli, Mario. "adidas Launches New adizero Feather." *Competitor* (Unknown), August 2, 2011, sec. Shoes and Gear. http://running.competitor.com/2011/08/shoes-and-gear/adidas-launches-new-adizero-feather_34179.

39. "Imagine If We Could Grow Clothing. . . " Biocouture. http://www.biocouture.co.uk/.

40. Betancourt, Gaspar. "3D Printing: Billion Dollar Industry Almost Ready to Go Mainstream." *WB Engineering* (Miami), January 5, 2012, sec. 3D Printing. http://www.wb-3d.com/2012/01/3d-printing-is-a-billion-dollar-industry-and-is-almost-ready-to-explode-into-the-mainstream/.

41. *Kurzweil Accelerating Intelligence* (Unknown), "Advances in Nanotechnology Enable Targeted Drug Delivery," March 31, 2011, sec. News. http://www.kurzweilai.net/advances-in-nanotechnology-enable-targeted-drug-delivery.

42. Frucci, Adam. "Record Labels: Change or Die." *Gizmodo* (Unknown), March 11, 2010, sec. Music. http://gizmodo.

com/5481545/record-labels-change-or-die.

43. "TacTiles." InterfaceFLOR. http://www.info.interfaceflor.
com/content/diff-tactiles.

44. Patel, Prachi. "Water-Repelling Metals: New metals will
keep engines and turbines dry and ice-free." *MIT Technology
Review* (Cambridge), October 15, 2008, sec. Energy. http://
www.technologyreview.com/communications/21530/?nlid
=1428&a=f.

45. *J&O Fabrics Store*, "Fabric of the Future: Fabric That
Can't Get Wet," January 28, 2011, sec. Newsletters.
http://www.jandofabrics.com/newsletters/fabric-of-
the-future-fabric-that-cant-get-wet/.

46. Colvin, Jill. "Scientist Wants to Bring Nanotechnology to
Garment District." *DNAinfo* (New York), August 2, 2011, sec.
Midtown. http://www.dnainfo.com/20110802/midtown/
scientist-wants-bring-nanotechnology-garment-district.

47. "Rachel Botsman: The Case for Collaborative Consumption." TED: Ideas Worth Spreading. http://www.ted.com/
talks/rachel_botsman_the_case_for_collaborative_con-
sumption.html.

48. See, for example, http://www.bagborroworsteal.com/welcome;http://www.carsharing.net/;http://bike-sharing.blogspot.com/; http://www.urbangardenshare.org/; http://www.seglet.com/.

49. Crotti, Nancy. "Some Corporations Looking for Tenants to Fill Extra Office Space." *Minneapolis St. Paul Business Journal,* October 10, 2010. http://www.bizjournals.com/twincities/stories/2010/10/11/focus4.html.

50. Pearce, Fred. "The End of the Road for Motormania." *New Scientist* (Unknown), August 16, 2011, sec. Opinion. http://www.newscientist.com/article/mg21128255.600-the-end-of-the-road-for-motormania.html?full=true.

51. Bobkoff, Dan. "The 'Google of Manufacturing?' One Company Shows a Possible Future." *WBEZ 91.5* Chicago, September 7, 2011. http://www.wbez.org/story/%E2%80%9Cgoogle-manufacturing%E2%80%9D-one-company-shows-possible-future-91592.

52. You can read more about the science behind Sharklet at http://www.sharklet.com.

THINK dMASS

*Exercises for Applying
dMASS Concepts*

Exercise 1:
Matching Products and Functions

This exercise is designed to help you think about products and functions in a different way. You'll need scraps of paper and a pen or pencil. The exercise works best with a small group of people.

Each person should write down the name of an object or product on one side of a piece of paper. On the other side write one word that describes what the item does or a benefit it provides. For example, if you chose a disposable, compostable cup, benefits could include: portability, convenience, protection from heat, soil amendment, etc. Each product may have multiple functions or benefits, but there should be only one function or benefit on each piece of paper. You will need multiple papers for each object. Repeat this step several times with different objects, including your company's products.

- When you're done, spread out all of the papers with the function side facing down. Now, organize the cards into groups of objects that you think have similar functions or benefits. Which objects did you group together? Flip the cards over to reveal the functions. Are the functions of the objects you grouped together similar? Record your findings on a sheet of paper.

- Spread out the papers again, this time with the object side facing down. Now group related functions together, and then flip the papers over. Are you surprised that certain products have similar functions? Are your groupings any different than the first round?

Notes

_____

_____

_____

_____

_____

_____

*Recognizing the need is the primary
condition for design.*

Charles Eames

Exercise 2:

Opportunities with New Materials

This exercise is designed to help you think about the relationship between materials and functions. Materials science is a rapidly evolving field. How often do you rethink the materials in your products or purchases? Are you using materials that deliver the desired functions with the fewest tons of resources? Are you aware of new materials that could revolutionize your products (or give your competitor an advantage)?

- Choose a product you design, sell, or use.

- What are the functions of that product?

- What materials are currently incorporated into the product to deliver those functions?

- Now try exploring different materials online. You can search with keywords related to the functions you've identified here, terms specific to your product, and keywords such as "innovative materials" or "smart materials." You can also use keywords such as biomimicry or nanotechnology, or start by browsing websites dedicated to materials science or to new technologies. When you find interesting articles or websites, think about how these materials are being used and what other possible ways they might be used.

- Do you see a potential match between materials in development and the functions you need in your product?

- What could you do now regarding higher-performing materials? For example, could you research a material you identified to see if it has potential for use in your product? Could you substitute a material in your product? Could your company participate in research and development of a material? Could you simply follow on-going developments in the materials you identified?

Notes

Business, more than any other occupation, is
a continual dealing with the future;
it is a continual calculation, an
instinctive exercise in foresight.
Henry R. Luce

Exercise 3:
The dMASS Multiplier

Being more aware of the resources involved in bringing a product to market makes it easier to see opportunities for minimizing resource use and costs. This exercise is designed to help you understand how savings in one part of a product's life cycle can affect every other part. For example, you can explore how savings in manufacturing can result in savings in the entire supply chain.

- First, choose a product.

- Write down everything that goes into that product, starting with water and fuels.

- Think about the interrelationships among the resources. Delivering water requires energy; generating energy requires materials, which in turn require additional resources to extract from our environment. Each resource input leads back to other resource inputs. Keep writing them down.

- When you've exhausted your list, step back and reflect. Did your brainstorming lead to surprising places?

- Now go back to the item you started with and your initial list of resource inputs. If you could eliminate or reduce the need for one resource input, how would that change ripple through all of the resource requirements in the product's life cycle?

- Take one more look at your initial list. Is there one resource that's most vulnerable to supply disruptions or unpredictable price fluctuations? Is this is good place to start thinking about how to minimize inputs?

Notes

*You uncover what is when you
get rid of what isn't.*
R. Buckminster Fuller

Exercise 4:
Removing Functions

Each ingredient of a product has a primary function, a benefit. But it may also have other, undesirable characteristics. That's the idea we're exploring in the following exercise:

- Start by choosing a product that your company buys or sells.

- Make a list of all the materials you can think of that are in the product.

- What are the desired functions of each of the ingredients in the product you chose? Do they affect the product's appearance, durability, and effectiveness?

- What are the ancillary functions of those ingredients? Are those functions beneficial? Are they outdated? Are they really needed to deliver naked value?

- Given what you've learned in this book, is there an alternative (a different ingredient or an alternative product, depending on whether you chose a product your company sells or a supplier's product) that more closely matches the *benefits* you desire from the product with the *functions* of that product's ingredients? In other words, is there something that *delivers what you want* and *not what you don't want?*

Notes

*A designer knows he has achieved perfection
not when there is nothing left to add, but
when there is nothing left to take away.*

Antoine de Saint-Exupéry

Exercise 5:

Delivering Benefits Invisibly

In an ever-growing number of cases, there are innovative solutions that deliver benefits invisibly or in an entirely new way that eliminates the need for certain physical products. Here are two examples:

- Not many years ago, holding a face-to-face meeting with colleagues stationed in different places necessitated travel. Now, with video-conferencing, you can accomplish many of the same tasks without expending the resources associated with travel.

- Self-healing and responsive materials repair and rebuild themselves without additional resources. Self-healing paint was recently introduced for cars and mobile phone cases. As applications of this technology expand, it's possible that continual upkeep of house paint, for instance, could become obsolete.

Think of three ideas to replace current products with something that delivers the benefits of

those products in a different, near-invisible way. This
exercise is about challenging norms and coming up
with creative solutions, even if they seem at first to
be impractical or unrealistic. Let go of your present assumptions and presumed constraints. Imagine how a technology or strategy from other fields
could apply to your products. As you think, focus on
the benefits that products deliver, not the products
themselves.

Notes

I've never felt like I was in the cookie busi-
ness. I've always been in a feel good business.
My job is to sell joy. My job is to sell happi-
ness. My job is to sell an experience.

Debbi Fields

Exercise 6:
Aiming for Naked Value

Let's revisit an exercise from the book. Choose a different product from the one that you used for this exercise in the book and think about how you can move it closer to naked value.

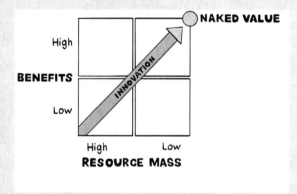

(A) Identify the baseline benefits and resource mass of your product. Create a very simple description of what core benefits your product provides to customers and then jot down a list of the major resource inputs for the product.

(B) List several ways you could reduce the product's resource inputs while retaining benefits.

(C) List several ways you could increase benefits while keeping resource inputs the same.

(D) Identify potential strategies that reduce mass *and* increase benefits.

Now use the product categories A-D to describe what your product might look with different performance improvements, and describe your product in its naked value form.

Notes

*There's a better way to
do it. Find it.*

Thomas A. Edison

dMASS

Leadership through resource performance

Sign up for the
dMASS newsletter

Request a speaker
or workshop leader

Explore dMASS
innovation examples

Watch fun &
thought-provoking videos

Read articles from
dMASS.net contributors

Connect & share

Connect with us at
www.dmass.net

 @dMASS_net

 facebook.com/dmass.net

CPSIA information can be obtained at www.ICGtesting.com
Printed in the USA
LVOW132153100812

293922LV00007B/48/P

9 780985 447403